Demimonde

by Kierstin Bridger

Lithic Press
Fruita, Colorado

Demimonde
Copyright © 2016 Kierstin Bridger

Design and layout: Harvey-Rosen

Demimonde
Kierstin Bridger
ISBN 978-0-9962170-4-0
Lithic Press

LITHIC PRESS
fine books for an old planet

www.lithicpress.com

For all the women who shone in the half world.

*For those who reinvented themselves when wisdom hit
and for all the forsaken who fell under the weight
of unspoken days.*

Table of Contents

Ella Undone and Paraphrased   13
Demimonde   17
Mining Town   21
Mattie's Breach   25
What Flourishes In the Dark   29
Ella Names Them All "God"   33
Bawdy House Brawl   37
Back Alley   41
Ella Said Hunger Is the Villain   45
Carmine   49
Forced Branches   53
Hey, You There   57
Ella's Dress of Faith   61
Relic   65
Alley Flowers   69
Ella Belladonna   73
Telluride Marshall   77
Ella Unrequited   81
Baby Names   85
What Flourishes In the Dark   89
Ascendant of Shadows   93

Demimonde

Ella Undone and Paraphrased

I love it most when I am adored.
Men kneeling as I stand,
eyes cast upward, trembling
even when their hands are rough,
I know my flesh is a lavender balm.

Once a boy warmed my nipples
again and again just to witness
their pucker at cool air,
his fledgling whiskers,
or the passing of his thumb.

Worship is more curious than
their quick release—
my face turned to the wall,
mine-dust etched in the well
of their chewed fingernails.
I grip tight against the ticking,
their breath, the exhale of cold tunnels,

the greasy smell that lingers
from their Welch lunch—sharp taste of tin.
They are gone before I can tie my wrap,
smooth my hair, return to steady breath.
That urge I know. Nameless, I understand.

Demimonde

Is it any wonder she calls
to children from her lace curtains,
to fetch her pharmacy cures,

ergot dust and oil of tansy,
prussic acid and laudanum
to ease the void?

Black thread to web
frayed stockings,
white to repair a torn chemise.

She lives in a West
where larkspur seeds
are sought for poison,

where fellow fair Cyprians
dab belladonna beads on closed lids,
where bedroom eyes blink narcotic

for rough men and fine—
men who sift gold dust
in their pockets,

who once upstairs,
call her by the third name
she'll conceive this year.

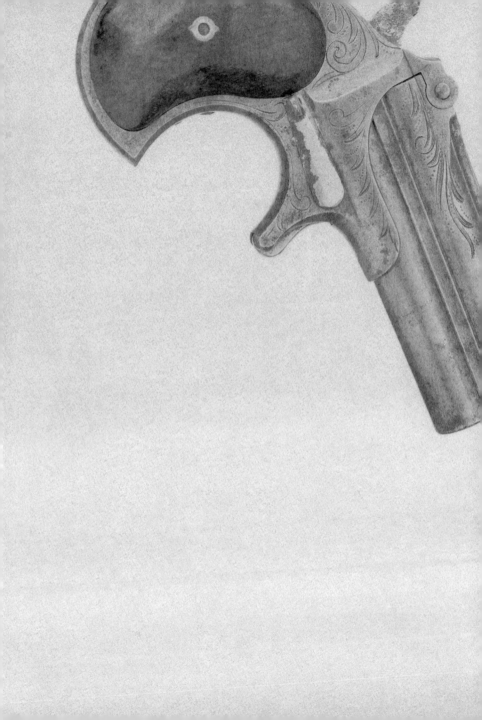

Mining Town

Lightning breaks open the heart of the wood
        every manner of seed takes root
whether by swallow or scavenge,
        by hawk or by hoard.

This is what it feels like to be haunted
by the carved bars, vaults, and walls of this town.

In the attic overhead, a heaving chest
breathes-in fine dust like powder.

It's almost imperceptible this slow drag,
curling photographs of the sporting life,

tokens unspent, brittle lace gone to moth
fodder and waste. A town bought on backs.

Museum portraits catch my eye as I walk,
their milky violet bottles, child-sized shoes,

and in the alleys, colt shells unearth
under most any cloud-kick of dirt.

Stepping out into the wild, the river talks too.
They were too young to be forgotten,

pine-hearted sirens, rustler husbands
banking on their brides, runaway maids

farming their babies to the retired, "one night wives,"
women hobbled by the work, olden and hidden.

so many mine smudged doves—
broken-winged birds waylaid by the boom.

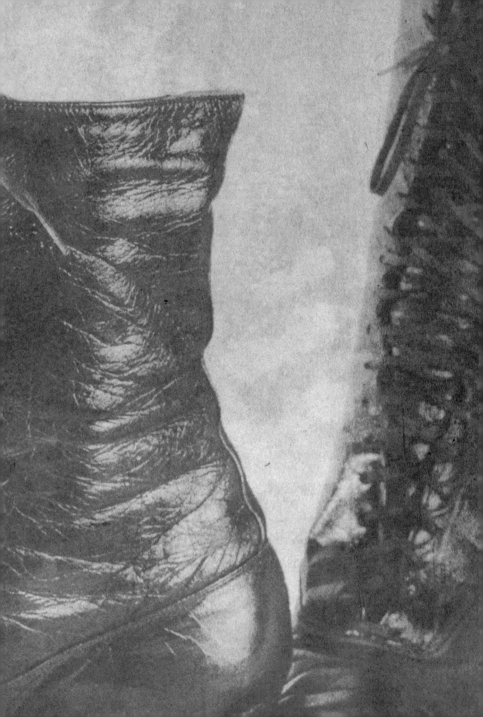

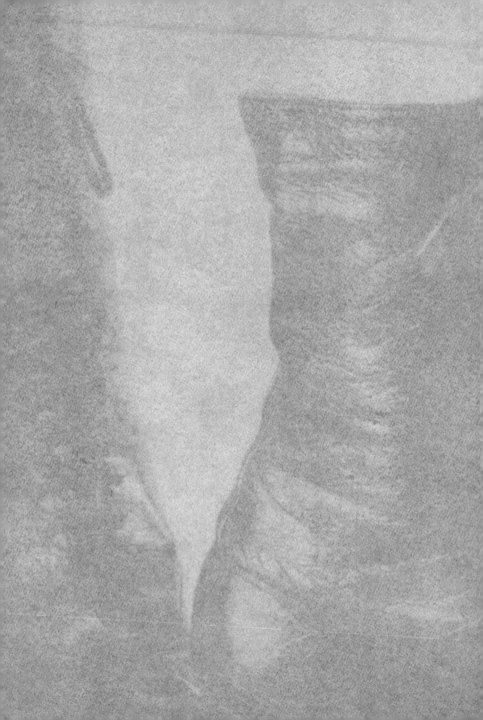

Mattie's Breach

No one knew who I was that first Sunday.
I strode through the neighborhoods in fine yellow silk
assuming all the townspeople at church.
The chapels have clear panes it seems.
Boys were watching me, asking questions.
Wives and priests don't want reminded
there is a second world.
Respectable was never a hat
I could afford comin' up.
This trade is mother-taught,
ask my sisters,
this old profession
keeps my hands clean and my heart boot-black.

What Flourishes In the Dark

Ella, 24

In the parlor house,
room number seven,
Ella would hang a wreath of garlic.
To provide stamina, she said,
to keep her loyals strong.
Too potent at the beginning of the tryst,
she warned, but she knew a nibble
for the amble home would mask
the taste of her on his mouth—
perhaps his wife would assume a sauce.

Ella Names Them All "God"

I turn nun
at twilight—
my genuflection:
bare knee
to clotted boot,
hallowed rituals
mouth open to seed,
to the urgent weeping
of the body.
My opiate visions:
a cool brook,
a trout-striped tongue.

My skin is tithe
for my madam,
for powder,
strong spirits
and bribes.
My body
taken crumb by crumb
for communion,
for a confession box.
Do you hear me call,
Oh God, Oh God?

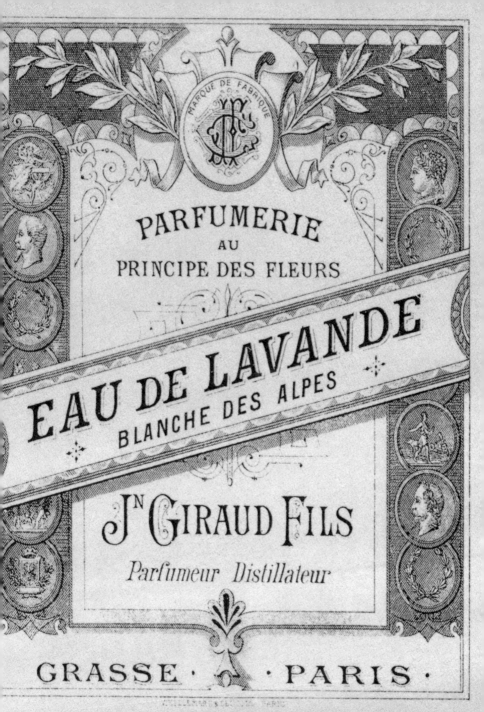

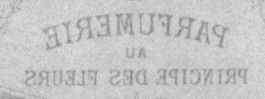

Bawdy House Bawl

This is the land
where ladders fall away,
when your derringer's sold

and the rent's overdue.
No more candied violets
and French perfume.

It's filched tinned peaches
the moment your child is born.
You'll watch your wild rose

choke on the last rung—
you'll work the crib,
you'll work the line.

Back Alley

Down the line morphine completes the day.
Not the sort of place young girls start
but where they end their blush, for good.

You heard of Leadville,
where women live tucked away
shaded from the glare of society,

bathed in the glow of the railroad
man's lantern, tobacco spittoons
too fine when the floor will do.

In back of these rough-shod houses lie
a place they christened *Stillborn Alley*
where ghosts rise up in eerie song.

Can you hear the wavering sound,
like an S-curved saw blade, missing teeth,
played over a lap with a rosin coated bow.

There are no wooden crosses there
only wandering, climbing vines,
thorns which stray from beyond fences,

seeds sprung from backstreet blooms.
These hard runners root while boot–trod weeds
mass on the sinking, mud-rutted mounds.

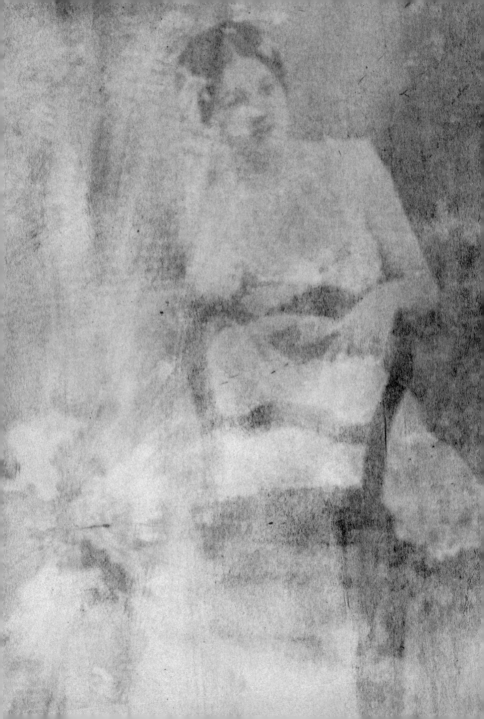

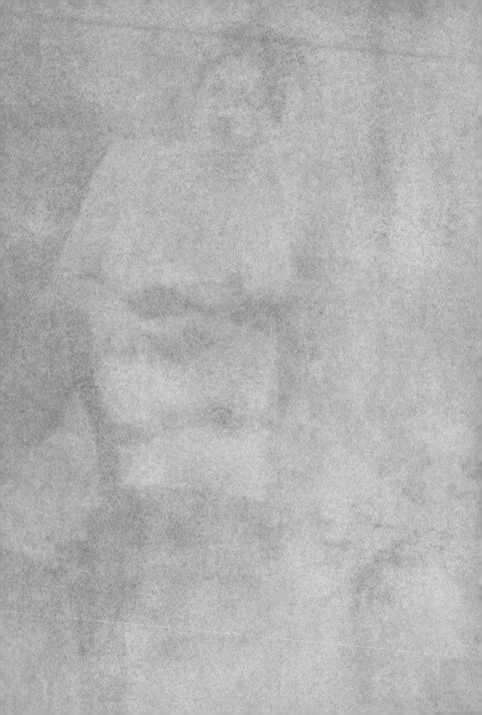

Ella Said Hunger Is the Villain

I'll tell you about the bashful ones:
    Their pink cheeks pay for a brute's slaps.
        They don't know my thigh hoax:
            the clenched bait and switch,
                how I even the score.

Every virgin farm boy: peaches on the bottom bough.
    My mother was poison after men lashed her,
        felt the same hot rush of sway
            when the whiskey trued her tongue.

You don't know the comfort of rags, sir,
    until you've bared your sharp, ravening ribs,
        beat back your black winged wrap,
            again and again, to bare your naked breast
              — to November's door.

Carmine

He sliced my smile wider
and when I fought back
they fined me for disorderly conduct.
I lost my saloon girl position
worked the fine off on my knees.

      Pale white powder
      and the precise shade of lip rouge
      will conceal for an evening or two
      but fantasy is built
      from flawless specimens.

Orchard red, sweet to the core,
ripe for the gluttonous worm.
A man will pluck an unspoiled apple
from bent branch, devour half and,
juices dripping, toss the rest.

Forced Branches

Doc brought sticks last March,
said, *Maybelle, they'll cure yer blues.*
Had to keep water in the jar,
had to watch 'em everyday.

Doc was 'fraid I'd poison myself again.
Sure he'd find that laudanum bottle clean,
and the floor wet with my sick.

I wake up every day sore-limbed and wrung-out
but damn if that branch don't live—
every knuckle split green.

And today, I woke to afternoon sun,
tens of tiny yellow stars,
velvet and fresh
gapin' them love eyes at me.

Hey, You There

*"Love is a cunning weaver
of fantasies and fables."*
　　　　　　　–Sappho

You haven't heard my voice.
What is it you want to know—
that it feels like factory work?
That I can't get enough?

We walk only the shade-rich side of the street.
Beauty comes to us, Handsome, *house calls*,
Get it? Cat house, cat calls.

I ain't political. I'm a fighter.
I promise some, deliver more.
I'm not just a tart with a heart,
I'm an opportunist, speculator, a chancer.
Keep your eyes on the fringes, boy.
I'll hold your cards, I'll blow the dice.

I don't think about birthday cakes much
or the orphan train that led me here,
the way they checked my teeth,
the way they changed my name.
I don't think about the half-lie—
Not abandoned.

I had a mother back in Brooklyn.
The clergyman rounded us up,
all us lice-headed little thieves.
I had my mother's address in my grip—
Someone stole it while I slept.

My eye's on the coin, Handsome,
let me see your hands.
I'll bathe you first then me.
You have fine paws— by the by—
rugged and strong,
I never seen the like.

I have a husband, a gambler in his own right.
If you'd rather, I have no one in the world
but you tonight, I've got more truths
to whisper but it will cost extra.
Isn't your head held high
worth every penny, every silver dollar?

Six girls on the line tonight,
in a slow, snow-molded December.
We each have our own debt.
No doubt we'll knock each other out,
just to scratch the post—

My real name? No.
Cat got my tongue.
If you come see me again,
Handsome, I'll let her out.

Ella's Dress of Faith

The moon makes lace of the landscape.
Top branches frill on the cuff of midnight.

There's a white church beyond the tall elm
and the shadows of men lurk after hours,

faceless suits, hands pocketed, reading
matchbooks blind. While under a scrolled gable

lies a simple window, half black, half white.
Above the door only the lintel is dry-wood gray,

darker still the chalk-smoked gravel pathway.
Some nights I long to be courted in my Sunday best

but by morning I remember the hem has been let down
again and again and cannot rise past the curve of my hip.

Relic

All day it stays dead-tooth gray.
Flat light falls over switchbacks,
eleven feels like noon, feels like three.

September blush tarts the aspen,
a saloon girl's sashay through scrub oak.
Above tree line the mine tailings rust,
sink back to earth, mimic
the granite spine of the trail.

What's left of metal is thin, hole-pocked.
Time has fashioned brittle wafers of tin,
the color deep as ripest peach skin
on the very verge of bruise.

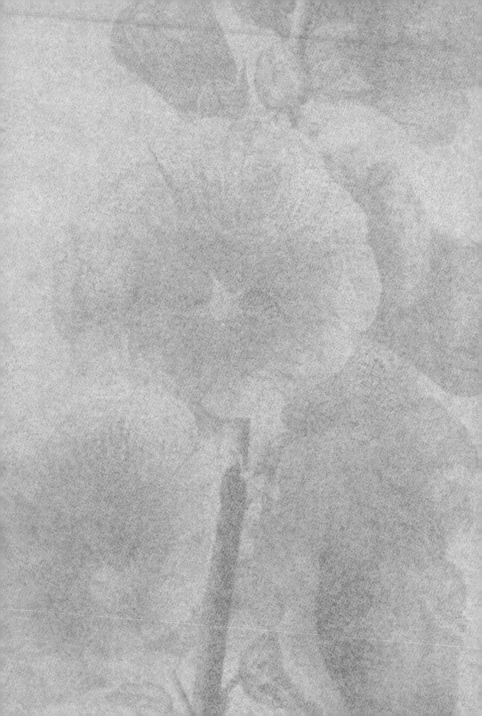

Alley Flowers

Gunshot holes through hollyhock leaves
broke my reverie,
broke it long enough to remember
the moon is not my mother
and my husband's never coming back—
the mine swallowed him whole, grubstake and all.

His pickaxe is not hidden beneath floorboards
though I sometimes pretend it is,
imagine I can wield it when sour breath
and stubble-scrape turn to blades.

One year all the men loved us,
fought to escort any woman under thirty—
negotiable virtue or not,
but we are now marked *not the marrying kind.*

I remember the lupine flags of early summer,
the night before I entered this perfume and taffeta house,
the sweet dandelion greens I had for supper,
the hot, salty bacon wilting them thin and dark.

I think of the hand-fed fawn at camp
when I pamper this stray amber-eyed tabby,
a gift I found under bullet-pocked leaves.
The gunpowder's scorched scent takes me back.

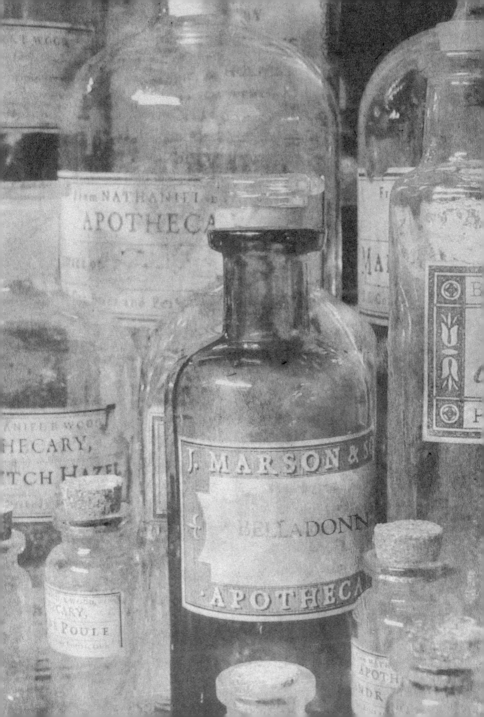

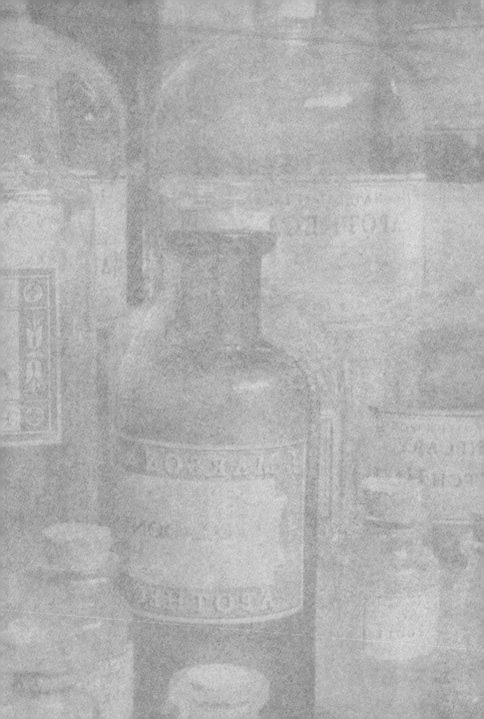

Ella Belladonna

My reflection on water, unlike the mirror's silver,
under the warbled veneer my girlhood erupts
as a cutthroat gasps for early spring.

To shock my tender fire out
I rattle my skull, spell my hair to the wind—
only to find it's gone ashes and cinder.

Broken and saddled by dusk,
cracked on the inside, deeper than bone
but to you, lover, I am the red sin of carmine—

the crimson dye made of the crushed body
of beetle scale— the glow
outside the papered window where I sit

preening my rosewood-scented neck,
stroking my mane with boar's brush,
one hundred licks to coax a blue raven shine.

I dilate my eyes, delude my senses—
drip by drop via apothecary dram.
Nightly my vision clouds us both.

Sweet ritual, glass and paint,
smoke and mirror to make a mask.
It's not water that slinks down my throat.

Vanity is an unstopped vial,
an unctuous master,
my trusted liquescent whip, my drug.

Telluride Marshal

It wasn't the way he spit when he passed
or trumped-up charges of vice.
It wasn't the reprimands he imposed in jail,
slaps and torn cloth, all the pots he wanted scrubbed,
pokes he insisted for free.
Not the cold water he dumped on our heads
or the way we scoured the cells on Sundays
to serve our sentence sham.

It wasn't his scowl or his contempt
when our madam stood in the muck-furrowed thoroughfare
in her faded wrap. She wasn't trying to make him a John
but to attempt to converse in the light of day—
her old dog, doing as all dogs do— his daily constitutional.

It wasn't the way he shot her pug dead in the street.
It was how he walked on,
saying to his equally armed companion,
"Those whores, I will not abide the lot of them."
I remember her soft knees sunk into the mud,
as she reached to stroke her little pet.

Ella Unrequited

He rode in on his haggard Palomino, eyes lit with stories,
prairie hardship behind the boast, enough coins for a bath
and a shave and just enough wind to tell his tales right.

In deep baritone he said his wife, lately departed, loved
to unlace her cotton gown, slip the fabric to her hips.
She'd shiver as she bared herself to the warmth of his back.

Labor was hard with no midwife, no coal for the stove, or water,
the well under two storms of snow. He cursed the hawks for their bid
at carrion feast as he pitched his pick through frozen earth.

After he buried his beloved and their unborn babe, he drained
the whiskey he'd hid in the barn. He found me
one evening at the dance hall bar, among the hurdy gurdy girls

with their calf length skirts, tassels and kid boots. I was a woman
who did what they wouldn't do. My only instrument the pluck
of my body, the curve of my ear, the rasp of my voice.

He followed my wavering key to a room above the saloon,
knew more trips downstairs meant I could make it another month.
Without word he stacked coin and paper in a circle like a clock.

I'll confess I'd die to lie most nights like that, in the dark rum scent
of his tonic and soap, the hollow of my stomach ladled
around the camber of his thigh, palms reaching toward the rise

of his chest, toward his steady heart. At first blush the damp
ache throb—my own sin in restless break— as he called out
in fevered dream to his darling, *Eugenia, I beg you to push, PUSH!*

If this were not a contract, and silver didn't seep
through our palms this ink-smudged morning, what promises
we might have let slip, but when I roused him at sunrise,

to point out the dawn, I saw our bond was etched in fading hoarfrost—
through winter's pane— our doubled-yoked grief. I saw myself
rouge-smudged, ruined dowry, moon-wrought at best.

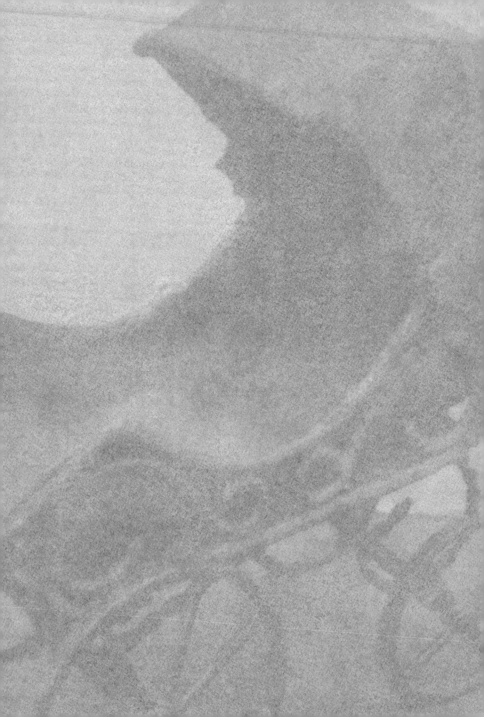

Baby Names

Muddy, slanted floors, rooms of narrow snears,
the one bent wood rocker in the corner,
light filtered through stained glass—
nothing pastoral or Magdalene, only
bright and pointed harlequin squares.

Gone are the soiled doves,
exchanging favors for the wages
of silver mines, rattled tales
and hymns, infantile endearments,
Dolly, Lamb, Lil Pistol, Sunshine.

Found in the bordello's attic:
pasted portraits in sepia, shape of a cradle,
a painted oak steamer trunk
storing infant gowns,
too far-gone to ever christen a child.

I think of the long stares, snowcaps
beyond the flies and their prism wings
which beat against the slipped and warbled glass.
Forgotten women whose whiskey hours drown
in kerosene-lit cribs lining this mining town.

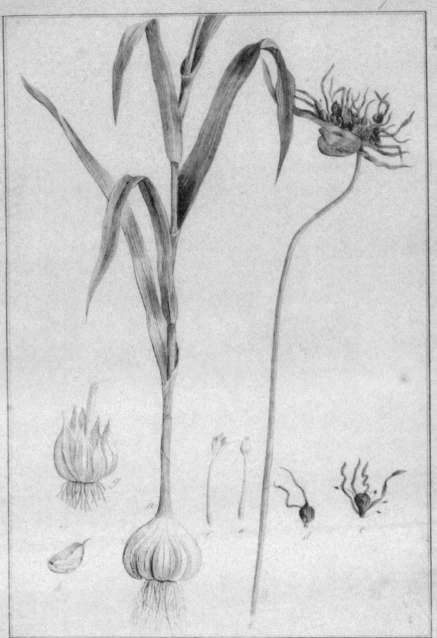

Allium sativum Lin.

What Flourishes In the Dark

Ella, 42

A basket at her door left in the rain,
wet garlic skin, crisp paper
now sodden, a familiar scent.

Her Ama wore bulbs like amulets.
Ella refused the old way,
neck wrung with children and allium.

We were toothsome once,
she said to no one.
I bit shoulders just to see my marks.

A sharp fragrance lingers:
rock-bound earth,
thin layers of protection,

the whole of its promise,
its solid, knuckled mass—
humble and domestic.

She longed for slow-cooked hours.
Deep, warm flavors unspooled,
silent nights, his index finger tracing hers,
eyes open under sun-soaked linen sheets.

To build a full life one must cleave
the half, toss the bitter, middle place.
Words stick to the meat of this savory false-fruit,
parchment clung, this salt-licked span, illegible.

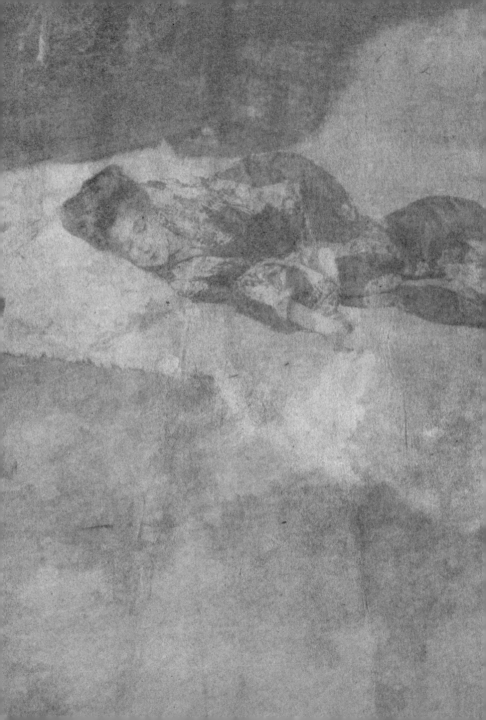

Ascendant of Shadows

The first wails I heard,
ghosts biting at the heels—
specters shrill in death as in life.

    It wasn't just tricks they had to earn—
    the price they could fetch for favors,
    hard liquid sell,
    the slick tongue they struck,
    songs that earned their supper.

Ella's presence was most eloquent;
the air hung with her oak-cask laugh,
smoky, ruby cut perfume,
the stain of her cinnabar pout,
rustle of silk on steps, lines of lyric patois,
heel clicks, and silver echoes, her rings on doorframes.

    There were others, in glassy ersatz jewels—
    coarser women, nipping from novelty flasks,
    cackling through graying teeth,
    skirts of quiet wool, thunderous corsets,
    and hair beneath tight, misaligned wigs.

This Demimonde, this underworld,
a state of liminal shadow,
of being sought in the dark,
banned in light,
of listening to voices living in cedar,
in the ashen white of aspen.

It's the blur we catch:
our other selves,
selves we'd want saved—
Perched as they are
in the glossy corner,
the spark of our unwavering eye.

ACKNOWLEDGMENTS

With gratitude to my many teachers, especially Sandra Alcossar, Joseph Millar, Dorianne Laux, Leslie Adrienne Miller, Natalie Diaz, David St. John, and Ellen Bass. Thank you to the Literary Burlesque creator Amy Irvine McHarg who first conceived of the show which inspired me to give voice to these women. To the Monday Night Devotees of wild writing whose heart and passion know no end: Kerry Wilson, Ann Dettmer, Robyn Cascade, Colleen Gardner, and Leigh Robertson. Thank you to the Anne LaBastille Adirondack Writing Residency. Hats off to Darla Biel, Laurie Wagner, Wendy Videlock, Michael McCullough, Beth Paulson, Kyle Harvey and Danny Rosen for their vision and faith.

I am grateful to The Ridgway Chautauqua Society, the Ouray County Library, the Ridgway Library, The Ah Haa School and the Telluride Historical Museum especially Anne Gerhard. I could not do without Lana Dimmitt, Maureen O'Driscoll, Heather Yeowell, Ginny Woo, Kari Kelly, Gretchen Ferazza, Stephanie Wallin, Genee Bolton, and Sam Roxas Chua for friendship and encouragement. To Jenny Robertson and Lisa Allen Ortiz for dreaming a little dream with me at Pacific.

I have enormous appreciation for Natasha Trethewey's *Bellocq's Ophelia* and to Beth and Jack Watson for their curiosity and generous nature.

Finally, a deep bow to Leslie Vreeland of The Watch and Susan Viebrock of Telluride Inside and Out who championed my work and printed several early versions found in this book.

Lastly to my most eager and first listener, Scott and our best thing: Sophia.

A portfolio of poems from Demimonde was selected as a finalist for the 2015 Manchester Poetry Prize.

Kierstin Bridger is a Colorado writer. She is a
winner of the Mark Fischer Poetry Prize, and
the 2015 ACC Writer's Studio Prize. She is editor
of *Ridgway Alley Poems*, Co-Director of Open
Bard Poetry Series, and contributing writer for
Telluride Inside Out. Her poetry also appears in
*Thrush Poetry Journal, Blast Furnace, The Hawaii
Review, Pilgrimage, Tulane Review, Fugue,* and
several anthologies. She earned her MFA at Pacific
University.

PHOTOGRAPHS

Bar Room, J.W. Swart's Saloon, Charleston, AZ, c1885 (p11)

Bird's eye view of Leadville, CO by J. J. Stoner, c1882 (p39)

Vintage photographic postcard, c.1904, uncirculated,
undivided back, publisher unknown, France,
Casas-Rodríguez Collection (p43 & cover)

Forsythia vividissima, Curtis's Botanical Magazine, c1851 (p51)

Orphan Train, Children's Aid Society Archive (p55)

Anna Held, Ziegfeld c1890s (p59)

Scrub Oak, Histoire des arbes forestiers de l'Amerique, c1812 (p63)

Hollyhocks, 19th Century Lithograph (p67)

Garlic illustration, K.K. Österr, c1841 (p87)

Evelyn Nesbit, Rudolf Eickemeyer, c1901 (p91)

PRAISE FOR DEMIMONDE

These are the songs of saloon girls and prostitutes working the mining camps of the old west— mocking and lyrical, forlorn, ragged, radiant with hunger and cruelty. Check out their clean lines and spikey language, their gunfire and laudanum and perfume.

–Joseph Millar, author of *Overtime and Blue Rust*

Kierstin Bridger amazes me with the pure energy that she is able to bring to everything in her life, including poetry. Seamus Heaney called poetry psychic fossil fuel, and Kierstin works that mine, pickaxing coal, finding diamonds. *Demimonde* is a collection about the dimly–lit world of women who sold their attention and bodies to survive the nineteenth century in the West. What sets Bridger apart as a poet in a densely populated literary world is not only her robust narrative, coupled with growing wisdom, but the way she is able to build , in a manner that often seems effortless, startling and unique clusters of language. I don't know another poet writing today who is able to fashion language into such radiant new symmetries. I look forward to watching her comet trail blaze forth into the world of poetry.

–Sandra Alcosser, author of *Except by Nature*
and *A Fish to Feed All Hunger*

This is an amazing collection of poems, spoken in the first-person voices of girls and young women who worked in the mining town "sporting houses" of Telluride around the turn of the last century. Kierstin Bridger's vivid, unsparing language captures the desperation, tedium and pathos of the day-to-day lives of these women in words and images that burn indelibly into the mind and sear the reader's soul like a branding iron. She has the poet's unerring eye for the minute, telling details that reveal not only the physical experiences of these women, but their acute, matter-of-fact perception of those experiences and their hopeless acceptance of the inescapable lives that encompass them. Ms. Bridger so fully and intimately inhabits these women, her poems are not about them, they are of them and from them.

–Jack H. Watson, White House Chief of Staff,
Carter Administration